Preface:

Dear Reader,

The Workbook, "*The Red Diary Program – Welcome to the Savage World of Branding*" is all about Branding. This Workbook revolves around a set of Exercises which will take you through the process of Branding at various levels including Personal Branding.

After many years of successful professional career, creating and handling multiple Brands at multiple levels, I envisioned to create this Workbook so that anybody who is interested in the Science and Art of Branding can get a sufficient exposure through practical exercises mentioned in this workbook.

Once the exercises mentioned in this Workbook is completed, the reader will get thoroughly exposed to the Savage but highly exciting World of branding.

As this is a Workbook which I have completed myself, I would be available to guide the readers through the exercises mentioned in this Workbook.

You can reach me at sanjaynair005@gmail.com for any queries or guidance required for completing this Workbook.

With Best Wishes and Regards,

Sanjay Nair

About the Author:

Sanjay Nair is a Professional Consultant with more than 16 years of Experience in the field of Marketing and Commercialization. After working with reputed companies Nationally and Internationally, Sanjay Nair now runs his own Consulting firm in Hyderabad, India.

You can reach Sanjay Nair at his email id: sanjaynair005@gmail.com

Contents:

The Red Diary Program - The Savage World of Branding

Introduction:

The "Red Diary Program- The Savage World of Branding" is for one and everybody who lives in this world now. It introduces you to the world of branding at your Personal level as well as at the level of marketing Products and Services and Corporate branding as well.

Through the exercises of Red Diary Program Workbook, you would be able to learn and relearn everything about branding in the context of today's cut throat competition.

I. **It's a Savage World out there:**

Whether we like it or not, it's a savage world out there. Everybody is trying to put themselves in an advantageous position so that they can earn more, spend more, and enhance their reputation at their professional and social spheres of life. In this kind of world, becoming generic commodity is like dying before your actual death. This is a world of cut throat branding where standing out from the crowd is more than important. Disruptive Brands exactly do that. Disruptive brands break existing Boundaries and create altogether newer platforms to work with. These are the game changing Brands.

Let's do an exercise to ascertain the savagery of the disruptive branding around us.

Exercise 1: Study the bellow mentioned 25 Brands and make notes on how these 25 Brands changed the game altogether through disruptive branding.

1. Uber
2. Airbnb
3. Facebook
4. Red Bull
5. Snapchat
6. Alibaba
7. Netflix
8. Under Armour
9. Instagram
10. Apple
11. CVS
12. Taylor Swift
13. Google
14. Warby Parker
15. Chipotle

16. 72andSunny
17. SoulCycle
18. Rent the Runway
19. Houzz
20. Waze
21. DraftKings
22. Coke
23. Eataly
24. Birchbox
25. Virgin America

II. Don't become another Generic:

As discussed before, being part of the crowd puts you in great disadvantage and you end up being type casted as a Generic. This is true at the individual level as well as at the level of a product or service or the corporate identity.

Let's do an exercise to avoid becoming a generic which leads to something called as Brand Genericide.

Exercise 2: Study the bellow 10 Brands and make notes on how these 10 Brands destroyed their own success through Brand Genericide.

1. Escalator
2. Thermos
3. Yo-Yo
4. Aspirin from Bayer
5. Xerox
6. Hoover
7. Taser
8. Rollerblade
9. Frisbee
10. Bubble Wrap

III. What is Branding?

Branding gives an identity. Branding is essential to project certain unique offerings which may be of interest to the targeted set of audience. Branding gives you an aura and protects you from falling into the world of generics.

Let's do an exercise to understand the process of Branding.

Exercise 3: Study the bellow 10 Brands and make notes on how these 10 Branding Examples made it big in their own ways

1. Apple
2. Pixar (or Disney/Pixar)
3. GE
4. 3M
5. Coca Cola
6. BMW
7. Visa
8. McDonald's
9. UPS
10. Nike

IV. What is the Difference between a Brand and a Product?

A product is an offering with specific features and benefits to satisfy some particular needs where as a Brand goes beyond ones needs in the sense that it creates an association value to the user of the brand. The user of the brand experiences benefits which are tangible as well as intangible.

Let's do an exercise to understand the difference between a Brand and a Product.

Exercise 4: Study the bellow 8 Brands and make notes on how the bellow 8 Brands exemplify the difference between a Brand and a Product:

1. Handbags Vs Gucci
2. Wrist Watch Vs Rolex
3. Sports Shoes Vs Nike
4. Sports Shoes Vs Reebok
5. Coffee Vs Starbucks
6. Perfume Vs Armani
7. Sun Glasses Vs RayBan
8. Smart Phones Vs Apple

V. Brands around you - Analysis

Today Brands are created in the digital world as well. The world of branding has expanded exponentially.

Let's do an exercise to analyze major "digital" brands around us.

Exercise 5: Study the bellow Hot List: The 24 Digital Phenomenon that Defined Branding

1. Snapchat
2. Periscope
3. Netflix
4. BuzzFeed
5. Bleacher Report
6. Taco Bell
7. The New York Times
8. Apple Watch
9. YouTube
10. Funny or Die
11. Transparent
12. Comedians in Cars Getting Coffee
13. Casey Neistat
14. Instagram
15. Taylor Swift
16. Kik
17. Amazon
18. Tinder
19. Spotify
20. Whisper
21. Uber
22. Snapchat
23. Metal Gear Solid V: The Phantom Pain
24. Clash of Clans

VI. Case studies from Branding World:

Case studies from the world of branding are very exciting to study whether it be Corporate branding or branding of a Product or Service or branding of people.

Let's do an exercise with Case studies from the branding world.

Exercise 6: Study the bellow mentioned 11 Brands and make notes on how these 11 Brands stood the Test of Time

1. Twinings

2. The New York Times
3. Beretta
4. Tiffany & Co.
5. Baker's Chocolate
6. Mercedes-Benz
7. Fruit Of The Loom
8. Levi Strauss & Co.
9. Jim Beam
10. Colgate-Palmolive
11. Brooks Brothers

VII.   You are a Brand:

The advent of the digital world has forced us to portray ourselves as Brands. When there is so much information about so many people around us, personal branding will help us stand apart at least in things that we are good at. This will also prevent us from falling into the world of generics where we simply become part of the crowd.

Let's do an exercise to understand our personal branding potential.

Exercise 7: Study the bellow mentioned examples of Personal Branding and see how Personal Branding helps to develop your overall personality

1. Tony Robbins
2. Amy Cuddy
3. Jeff Weiner
4. Michelle Obama
5. Simon Sinek
6. Chip and Joanna Gaines
7. Richard Branson

Conclusion:

The Red Diary Program is all about branding. After going through the exercises of Red Diary Program, you are ready to unleash your branding potential in multiple ways. Welcome to the Savage World of Branding.

WORKBOOK EXERCISE SPACE: